DOES RAIN EVER FALL UP?

Contents

Written by Claire Llewellyn

Collins

Does rain ever fall up?

Yes, it does – well, sort of! Water on the surface of the earth is always rising up into the sky. This water is invisible, so we don't call it rain. But it's water and it's always there.

How does this happen?

Have you noticed how a puddle dries up on a sunny day? The water disappears almost in front of your eyes! The sun's heat is changing the water from a liquid that you *can* see into a gas you *can't*. The gas is called water vapour. It has no colour or smell, and it mixes with the air.

Did you know?
The amount of
water in the air is only
a tiny amount of Earth's
total supply. If it all fell as
rain, it would cover
the earth with about
2.5 centimetres
of water.

What happens to water vapour?

Every day, the sun heats the land, and the air above it grows warmer and lighter. It rises up into the sky, taking water vapour with it.
High in the sky, the air cools down. This makes the water vapour change into droplets of water. They make a cloud.

Why are some clouds darker than others?

The billions of droplets inside a cloud bump into one another, growing bigger and bigger. The larger the droplets, the darker the cloud.

Did you know?
A droplet of water inside a cloud is up to 1,000 times smaller than a raindrop.

Why does rain fall from the sky?

Clouds are full of water. As the droplets grow bigger, they get too heavy to float and fall to the ground as rain.

rain gauge

Why isn't rain salty?

Most of the water vapour in the air comes from the surface of oceans and seas. So, you might expect rain to be salty – but it's not!
When seawater changes into vapour, the salt is left behind in the sea.

How long does it take for water vapour to fall as rain?

Every drop of water that changes into water vapour rises up into the sky. In time, it returns to the earth as rain. The whole process takes about nine days.

So, that's why the rain falls down!

How long does it take a raindrop to fall?

Raindrops come in different sizes and fall from different heights. A typical raindrop takes about two minutes to reach the ground. Larger raindrops take less time; smaller ones take more.

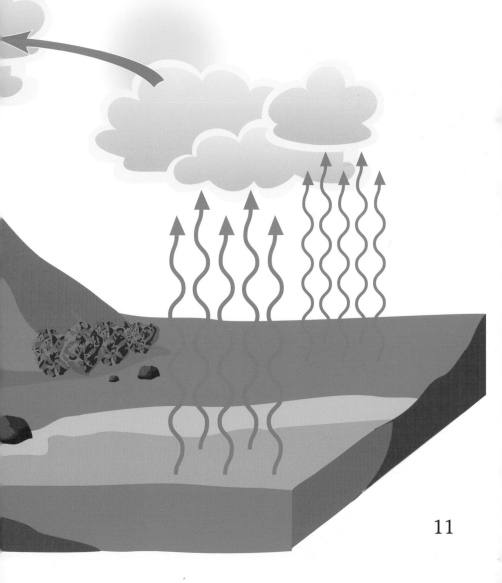

Where does all the rain go?

Most rain falls on the oceans and seas. After all, they cover nearly three-quarters of the surface of the earth. The rest of the rain falls on land. Some of it is sucked up by the roots of plants; some of it soaks into the ground. The rest runs into rivers and streams.

Did you know?
There is 15 times more water stored under the ground than there is in rivers and lakes.

Where do rivers and streams go?

Rivers and streams usually start high up in mountains and hills, as it rains a lot there! A tiny trickle will flow downhill. Other trickles join it and together they form rivers and streams. A river may flow for hundreds of kilometres as it makes its way to lower ground. Finally, every tiny trickle from the hills ends up in the sea.

What would happen if the oceans dried up?

Earth's oceans produce most of the water vapour that rises up into the sky and gives us clouds and rain. If the oceans dried up, there would be much less vapour in the air, and clouds and rain would be rare.
The shortage of water would turn the earth into a huge desert.

Did you know?
Most of the fresh water on Earth is found in the ice at the North and South Poles.

the South Pole

What if there was too much rain?

Too much rain can also cause problems. Swollen rivers burst their banks and flood the land. Floods wash away crops, destroy towns and can injure animals and people.

What if there wasn't enough rain?

All living things need water to survive. If there wasn't enough rain, very few plants would grow and animals could not survive. People need water every day to keep their bodies working well.

Did you know?
One in five people throughout the world lives in a place where water is **scarce**.

How can I save water?

Water is much too precious to waste.

Here are three things you can do to save it:

1. Turn off the tap while you soap your hands or brush your teeth.

2. Have showers instead of baths.

3. Turn taps off properly, so they don't drip.

Glossary

scarce a resource that there isn't much of

rain gauge a tube or funnel used to
    measure rainfall

Index

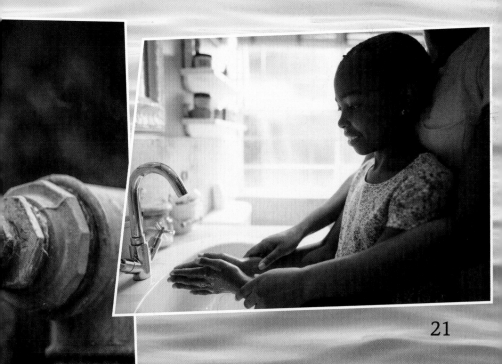

Water on the move!

Ideas for reading

Written by Christine Whitney
Primary Literacy Consultant

Reading objectives:

- discuss how items of information are related
- be introduced to non-fiction books that are structured in different ways
- discuss and clarify the meanings of words

Spoken language objectives:

- ask relevant questions
- speculate, imagine and explore ideas through talk
- participate in discussions

Curriculum links: Geography: Physical geography – weather patterns and the water cycle; Writing: write for different purposes

Word count: 786

Interest words: water vapour, floods, desert, swollen

Resources: rainstick or percussion instruments, paper, pencils, crayons and paints

Build a context for reading

- Ask children to talk to each other about being outside in the rain. Do they know how rain is formed?
- Encourage children to ask any questions they have about rain. Keep these questions and see if they are answered by reading the book.
- Read the title of this book together and discuss children's answers.

Understand and apply reading strategies

- Read pages 4 and 5 and ask children to explain to each other what *water vapour is*.
- Continue to read to page 11. Ask children to discuss the illustration using the following sentences: *The sun heats the land; The air above it grows warmer and lighter; It rises up into the sky, taking water vapour with it; High in the sky, the air cools down; The water vapour changes into droplets of water; They make a cloud.*
- Where is most of the fresh water on Earth to be found? Challenge children to find the answer to this question and give the page number where they found it.